Better Behavior Without Stress

Karen DeBolt, MA

MADHouse Publishing ♥ Hillsboro, Oregon

For my children, Talla, Molly and Sam who taught me more than I could have dreamed

For my husband, Dan, who helped me dream what is possible.

Table of Contents

Introduction

I've been writing on parenting topics for several years now, and I realize that most of what I write about comes down to just a few tools that I use over and over again. When I say use, I do mean use-- with my own children as well as my clients. Parenting is not simple—it's not like I have the magic wand that is going to make your children turn into perfect angels. Truthfully, I wouldn't even want to do that. For all of my worries and stresses with my son, I would not change a hair on his head. I laugh way more than I cry these days and that is what I wish for you.

This book is a compilation of all the tools that I have learned up until now. I will pass along my reference materials as I know them, and the counseling that I have gotten has been invaluable to this process. My hope is that this book will get you started on a path to discovering the best ways to work with your own children and with yourself.

Pat yourself on the back for all the hard work that you have done so far. Thank you for joining me on this adventure to calm the chaos in your home.

THAT'S IT! The moment of truth

When your car starts smoking and making that bad clunking noise or your water heater explodes leaving water all over the floor, you probably don't have any problem with calling a friend for advice or calling in the appropriate professional to help you solve the problem. No one usually feels shame if they can't do their own plumbing without help or fix their own car.

Yet, when an emotional crisis hits in a family or, even worse, an ongoing never ending list of challenges leaves us feeling exhausted, many feel too ashamed to ask for help. They feel embarrassed when the problem becomes apparent to friends or family or even that lady in the grocery store. Somehow they feel that they should be able to handle it themselves, without any help from anyone. They feel embarrassed that they don't "have it all together like everybody else."

When my son was 4 years old I was deeply in denial about our problems. He was getting more and more aggressive and his preschool teacher, a lovely woman who had worked with all my children for 6 years, finally threw up her hands and gave up. She said, "I just don't know what else to try. I'm very worried about him."

It was one of those, "That's it!" moments for me.

I knew that I had to swallow my embarrassment and get help for my family now. My shame had me in denial, and I couldn't afford to stay in that place anymore. So I went to see a professional and I learned a lot about what is often called, "Behavior

Modification." This was just the first step in a long journey, but it was important for me to stop feeling ashamed of being a "bad mother" and instead concentrate on learning new skills to parent a child who needed something different than I was able to provide up until then.

If there is one message that I hope my experience relates, it is "Don't wait!" The sooner you get the help that you need the sooner things will begin to be better for your children as well as yourself.

Are you having a "That's it!" moment?

Below are some signs and symptoms that it may be time to make a change. How many of these are true for your family? More than three "yes" answers may indicate that you have reached a "That's it!" moment too.

1. You find yourself avoiding certain social situations with your child because you are worried about your child's behavior.

2. You have friends or family members constantly giving you unsolicited advice about your child.

3. You are getting calls from school or day care about your child's problem behavior.

4. You find yourself losing your cool more than once a week.

5. You feel embarrassed by your child's behavior in public.

6. You feel hopeless about being able to make any changes because nothing seems to be working so far.

7. Your child seems to be either angry or sad much of the time each day.

8. You find yourself arguing with your partner about the best way to handle parenting your child.

9. You often find comfort in food or other unhealthy habits to relieve stress.

10. You are worried that your relationship with your child is beginning to suffer.

A challenge to face

You wouldn't be her reading this book if you didn't have a very challenging child who is hard to parent. You have already been doing everything that you know how to do, but even what works for your other children doesn't work with this child. You may have taken your child to the doctor, a psychologist or counselor, or even a psychiatrist. Yet, placing letters of diagnosis still don't necessarily help you with the very unique parenting skill set that you need to help your child be successful. Having your child attend a weekly or more commonly monthly session with a professional can be extremely helpful, but the bottom line is that you are there each and every day on the front lines. You are your child's best therapist.

Being your child's therapist

I remember when a psychologist first stated this concept to me. I was dismayed at the idea that I could be my child's therapist when I already thought that I was a horrible mother. The psychologist patiently explained that what works for an intense child like mine is different than what works for the typical kid. I knew this at a deep level because my daughters who are older than my son were so much easier to parent. The psychologist suggested some books to read and gave me some ideas to try. None of this was completely effective at first, but it began my journey to find effective parenting techniques that worked for me and for my child.

In order, to be effective you need a tool set to help you cope with the day-to-day situations that arise. You already have some tools so looking at the things that you are doing now that really work and getting rid of the things that you do that don't work would be a really good idea. Hopefully, there will be some new ideas here to help you decide what is not working and to tune up what is already working as well as new tools to add to your arsenal.

Your armor

You may think that because things at home are not going so well that you are not a good parent. The fact that you are here reading this book tells me that is not the case. You may keenly feel the judgments of family members, neighbors, teachers, church members, and even that old cranky woman at the grocery store. That shame and embarrassment is almost worse than struggling with your challenging child.

The fact is that these judgmental people do not have a clue how hard it is, and I want to support you to know that, yes, this is hard, exhausting work. I also want you to remember that this is not your fault. You didn't sign up for this and nothing you did caused it. That said, there are things that you can do that will help to make things better. Often the solution to a problem has nothing to do with the cause of the problem, and this is one of those cases. So, if someone handed you this book—I hope you will not see that as a criticism, but as a helping hand as it is intended.

Parenting a very intense, challenging child is not the same as parenting a typical child. Those skills simply will not be very effective. However what works for the intense child also works well for the typical child, so don't despair that you have to use two sets of rules and skills. Your typical child and your intense child will shine using the techniques that I explain in this book.

What not to do

Here are some ineffective parenting techniques that I would encourage you to particularly avoid in the future. This book will be giving you lots more techniques to take their place that are much more effective and will improve your relationship with your child rather than tear it down.

You don't need to decide today to give up techniques that you have been using, but I encourage you to at least take a moment to consider my reasoning and definitely try the new techniques that follow from here. You may find things shift without you making any decision about it.

Spanking

This is one of the most controversial parenting techniques. "Spare the rod spoil the child" is quoted by proponents; however, there has been study after study that shows that physical punishment is the least effective way to teach something.

With a challenging child, this is even more true. Many challenging children have a high pain tolerance. This means that you may have to really up the ante to even get a response. Aside from the dangers of this in terms of actually causing your child injury, which is a real danger by the time you have gotten the response that you want, the original issue at hand is no longer in his head at all.

So rather than "learn his lesson" about the behavior you are punishing, he learns that he "is bad" so he gets hurt. The behavior is not addressed at all so it continues. Sadly, many children will internalize the idea that they are "bad" even if you never use that word in your home. The child believes he is not worthy of love, so the bad behaviors continue. After all, what is the point of trying when he is just going to be in trouble again anyway?

Spanking does not give you the results that you want, and there are many better and safer ways to change behavior so that you don't have to worry about injuring your child or having child protective services darkening your door.

Warnings gone wrong

"I'm gonna smack you!"

My children's paternal grandmother is famous for saying this. Mostly she's joking, but not always. Rarely is she taken seriously by any of her 6 grandchildren and certainly never by her two children. Her saying this will make them laugh which might stop the behavior she is trying to stop, but mostly nothing changes . . . Threats and warnings simply don't work the way you might think.

Many times parents will yell out warnings or threats, which are often not ever carried out until the parent completely loses it, and deals out the big consequence.   Studies show that this type of parenting will actually increase the behaviors you DON'T want to see!

Example: John and the videogame

John has been glued to his video game for most of the day. His mom who has been busy all day working notices that he's in a trance with his thumbs moving so fast they are almost invisible. Mom says, "John go outside to play!" Then she starts doing the laundry and doesn't check on him for a while. When mom comes back ½ hour later, John is still there on the video game.

Now she threatens, "John stop playing now, or I'm gonna take that game away!" She goes to attend to the dinner in the oven. John continues playing and 15 minutes later John is still playing away on his game. Mom is yelling now, "John! John! Get off that now! I mean it!" John's little sister needs mom's attention so she goes to attend to her. John keeps playing. Mom returns and is beside herself. "THAT'S IT!" she screams. John says "Hey why are you yelling at me?" John now knows that mom has had enough, and he quickly turns off his game and rushes outside before Mom can yell anything about taking his game away again. Whoosh!

Selective hearing? Defiance?

By giving John multiple warnings mom has accidentally taught John to ignore her until her anger is at fever pitch. He learned at what point he needs to do what she wants without her carrying out her threat. For some kids, they will continue even to the point of getting the punishment because they are not able to read the signals that mom has had it and is about to actually carry out her threat now.

This is crazy making behavior for everyone involved. The child is frustrated because mom is yelling, and the mom is beyond frustrated because the child is defiant. This pattern can be very hard to break, but using the tools in this book, you will begin to see big changes very quickly.

Recipe for defiance

Both of these parenting techniques—spanking and threatening—are a recipe for defiance. They will negatively impact your relationship with your child and cause your child's defiance to escalate. Many children who are parented in this way will end up with more diagnosis letters like Oppositional Defiant Disorder (ODD) in addition to the others they may have.

Again, a typical kid may not respond in that way, but a challenging, intense child is going to push things to the limits of your patience. You need a specialized set of parenting skills that will work for your child in way that is firm as well as loving.

This is not working: Maybe its time to try something new?

Challenging child defined

There are some features, which seem to be common among hard to parent children. These features seem to defy any one diagnosis which is I think why it is so hard to pinpoint diagnostically what is going on. Children may be diagnosed with any combination of the following:

Attention Deficit Hyperactivity Disorder (ADHD), Attention Deficit Disorder (ADD), Oppositional Defiance Disorder (ODD) High Functioning Autism (HFA) Asperger's Syndrome (AS), Autism Spectrum Disorder (ASD), Pervasive Developmental Disorder Not otherwise Specified (PDD NOS), Non-Verbal Learning Disorder (NVLD), Depression, Mood Disorder NOS, Fetal Alcohol Syndrome (or substances) Bipolar Disorder, Anxiety Disorders, Obsessive Compulsive Disorder (OCD), Sensory Processing Disorder (SPD) and there are probably others . . .

My experience so far, such as it is, is that a child with multiple diagnoses is not necessarily in worse shape than another with one or none, but the professionals in the child life are struggling to fit a complex set of challenges into a specific diagnostic category.

In truth, the diagnosis that you need is the one that gets your child the services that he or she needs. That is the bottom line.

Some common features of hard to parent children that cross diagnostic categories:

- Executive Function Impairment
- Sensory Processing Challenges
- Social Skills Deficits
- Emotional Dysregulation

Not every child will have every feature listed but you may recognize many of these in your challenging child. These features will cross all types of diagnostic categories but are treatable nonetheless. Here is a brief description of the features, and a bit about how they affect your child's behavior.

Executive Function impairment

What you may notice:

Your child has almost no ability to prioritize, organize, or plan, which makes doing big projects extremely difficult including things like cleaning his room, doing homework, or the dreaded science project.

Her backpack looks like a bomb went off inside, and she forgets to turn in homework even though she spent hours completing it.

He may have big ideas with no real ability to handle all the details necessary or the persistence required to complete a big project.

She may have a hard time starting something, especially if she worries about whether she can do it "perfectly."

He may do things impulsively without thinking about the repercussions—this can be anything from climbing a tree or running in the street to hitting someone or doing some kind of self-harming behavior.

These types of challenges deeply affect your child's ability to be successful in school and in later life at work. The skills can be taught but it is a longer and more arduous process than a child without executive function delays will see. The frustration that comes with this may mean that your child will just give up sometimes. This may look like defiance at times.

The challenge for parents is to know when to allow natural consequences to teach the lesson and when to step in with a helping hand. Teaching the skills over and over is important, but after a point it will need to be up to your child to actually do what needs to be done. Yes, it will be hard to watch, but failing is a part of life for everyone, and sometimes failure is the best teacher.

Sensory Processing challenges

Some day Sensory Processing Disorder (SPD) may actually be a diagnostic category unto itself, but for now it is still in that murky undiagnosable area. Also, many people have only a few symptoms, which are manageable, but still increase stress levels. The really frustrating thing about sensory challenges is how a child may be "oversensitive" in one area and "under sensitive" in another area and some days those sensitivities will change without rhyme or reason.

So you may have a child who is "oversensitive" to the loudness of the cafeteria at school who will turn up his favorite video game to ear piercing levels and be happy as a clam. A child may shy away from light feathery touches, but crave deep pressure touches or vice versa. She may be able to ignore most smells, but become extremely agitated by the smell of artificial butter on microwave popcorn or become nauseous when exposed to Lilac or other smells that most people enjoy. This means that others are often invalidating these children's senses without even realizing the extent of the problem.

These difficulties create problems because of the unpredictability of the child, but also because it's hard for most of us to get how difficult something that we find enjoyable may be for our child. A typical day for one child might be a day of tortures for a child with sensory challenges. For example, here is a day that would send a child with a particular set of sensory challenges into a melt down guaranteed.

- Wearing jeans or clothes that are scratchy or have tags that scratch
- Eating in the very loud cafeteria at lunch time
- Smelling the special classroom treat of microwave popcorn or the teacher's cologne.
- Being in a classroom with fluorescent lights that buzz and appear to visually vibrate

Every child is different so this is just an example of how seemingly innocent things in normal everyday life can send a kid over the edge, and it makes no sense to the people around him or her. Often children with these difficulties are either not able to express them well verbally or have been taught that expressing them does no good, so they don't bother anymore.

Social skills deficits

A child with social skills deficits will have a very hard time knowing what is expected, understanding how his behavior affects other people, reading social cues, and initiating social interactions. He may say something that is considered rude in the context, but would be okay in another context, and then be confused about why he is in trouble.

Some examples of social skills deficits

John is sitting in grandma's parlor doing arm farts. Mom is mortified as Grandma gives her the eye. John is in big trouble now, but on the playground yesterday he was a rock star for his amazing arm fart skills. John is very confused because he doesn't understand why mom and grandma are so mad. He does it some more in hopes that they will laugh like the kids on the playground.

Shari wants to be friends with the other girls in the neighbor hood, but much to her dismay, they do not ask her to hang out with them. After some investigating, we discover that Shari has never said hello, initiated a conversation or even smiled at the girls in her neighborhood. She just expected that friendship would happen without understanding what she needs to do to initiate contact.

Other children at school and in the neighborhood are avoiding Andrew. Whenever he is with other children, he will take over the play and begin to boss everyone around. He may even become verbally or physically aggressive if he doesn't get his way. The other children now just avoid him or refuse to play with him all together.

Michaela is acting goofy at the dinner table. The family is having a nice meal together, and mom has worked very hard all day on cooking a healthy and flavorful meal. Michaela's dad is frowning at her and telling her to straighten up which she is ignoring. Michaela plays with her mashed potatoes and says that the "green beans are slimy and the meat is disgusting." Mom looks very upset now, but Michaela is oblivious that mom's feelings are hurt or actually that mom has feelings at all.

These scenarios illustrate how social skills deficits can cause children to appear to be "bad," "clueless," "without feelings," or even "mean" when in fact they are just delayed in learning what typical children learn without any instruction whatsoever. Social skills delays affect relationships within the family as well as with the outside world. A child that is seen as "mean," "unfeeling" "clueless" and even "aggressive" is going to be very challenging to parent as well as needing specialized instruction in social skills.

Children with social skills delays are more likely to be rejected by peers and struggle with being bullied and teased, which can affect their self-esteem dramatically.

Emotional dysregulation

Emotional Dysregulation refers to the inability to control emotions in an age appropriate manner—think of it as a frustration tolerance learning disorder. So when your 12 year old lies on the floor kicking his feet because he has to clean his room, he is displaying emotional dysregulation because those types of temper tantrums are more common for a three year old.

Where this gets particularly difficult is when you are dealing with these types of meltdowns every time your child becomes frustrated. This is enough to wear out anybody. It's tiring with a 3 year old, but you have hope that this is just a stage. Now it doesn't seem to be passing but getting worse and what about when he is a teen?

In truth, your child at this moment is probably not able to control his very strong feelings, or he would be doing that. Teaching emotional regulation is something that will have to be done over time, but in the meantime there are some tools that will help to reduce those meltdowns while teaching your child problem solving skills that will last a lifetime.

Now what?

Okay, so now that you have an idea about the types of challenges that your child faces, how do you change your parenting style to be more effective? Basically, slowly and one step at a time! If you try to implement everything in this book at once you will be running yourself ragged and setting yourself up to fail. However, I will teach some really effective techniques in this book, which will help you to take small steps to begin to parent your child in a way that gets results.

Each technique builds on the next. You may find, as I have, that by using these techniques, you almost never have to dole out a consequence. Your child will be happier. You will be happier, and the rest of the family will be happier. What could be better than that?

Collaborative Behavior Modification

Pure behavior modification works some of the time, yet sometimes with some kids, it will only make things worse. The reason for this is sometimes you are forcing a child to comply with a behavior that for some very good reason in the child's mind is completely unreasonable. The key to a behavior system that actually works is to have all the parties working together towards the goals. That means your child needs to be a part of the team as well!

This is where collaborative problem solving can really shine. You and your child work together towards a common goal that is satisfactory to both of you. Does that mean that you are giving in and letting the child run the show?

In a word, NO!

Both your concerns as the adult and your child's concerns are taken into consideration. Sometimes as the adult you will find yourself forcing the issue, but by taking your child's concerns into the equation you will find that your child will begin to be much more involved in the process, and therefore more compliant and invested in the outcome.

The really good part about Collaborative Behavior Modification is that all the parts of a good behavior modification program like specific praise, acknowledgement, setting the environment up for success, and clear expectations tend to work so well when done consistently that the consequences will rarely have to ever be given.

I will be introducing each part of the program individually, and I want to reiterate that all these parts work together in a way that makes it easy for your child to be successful and for you to keep up the good work! It's not easy to get started, especially if you were raised differently as most of us were.

The efforts you put in to make these techniques a habit will, without a doubt, create a better relationship with your child and less chaos in your home.

Specific Praise

"Not again!"

You just told your child for the 10,000th time not to jump on the couch, pull the cats tail or pester his sister. Why does he keep doing these things?! Is he trying to drive you crazy? It can sure feel that way, but in fact your child is not invested in how large your therapy bill is, and he has no idea how many times counting to ten has saved his life.

There is a better way to calm the chaos and have more happiness. I will describe how negative patterns begin, and how they get out of control. Then I'll explain a technique, which I have found to be key in reversing the negative behavior spiral. First, let's explore how those negative patterns got set in the first place.

A demand for more energy

Some people would say, "That child is just seeking attention." While attention does fulfill a need, there is more to the story. All humans require a certain amount of energy. This energy can come from many sources including other people, nature, and spiritual practice to name a few.

You have probably had the experience of feeling very drained after talking to a difficult person. This person may have been draining energy from you. Children also need energy and while some children are able to intuitively get energy themselves, others struggle to get their needs met without resorting to challenging behavior.

He doesn't care if the energy is positive or negative, he just knows subconsciously that he needs it and needs a lot of it.

So how does pulling the cat's tail fulfill this need?

When your daughter pulls the cat's tail, she receives an instant boost of energy from the cat's yowl. She then gets a second dose when you lecture her about how to treat the cat gently. With one fell swoop, she can get a double dose of energy. If she goes back and does it again five minutes later, you are probably going to lose your temper, which feeds this negative energy spiral even more.

When was the last time you got as animated about something good she did as you got when she did something that frustrated you?

It's human nature to take every day good behavior for granted. Isn't this the way it's supposed to be? You might remember to thank our child for a chore well done with a generic "good job" but in order to get a big energetic pay off your child has to do something pretty darn good. So, if you think about it, it's much much easier to pester a sister or jump on the couch.

To get the better behavior you want, you need to shift that energetic emphasis.

How to shift the emphasis

Simply put, the balance needs to shift so that negative behaviors receive a very matter of fact treatment – and good behavior receives animated, specific praise.

Specific Praise =
energy

This is not just "catching your child being good." This is actually creating situations where your child can receive praise. Praise does four things for your child:

- o Feels great!
- o Reinforces behaviors you want to see
- o Encourages even more good efforts
- o Strengthens your relationship

Mikey gets ready

Mikey was driving his mom, Arlene, and dad, James, bonkers with his constant arguing and back talk. His mom could say, "Mikey, lets go to the park." And he would have an argument every step of the way from putting on shoes and jacket to buckling his seat belt. Once he got to the park, he loved it, but it was so exhausting getting him there that Arlene didn't take him very often.

Someone suggested to Arlene that Mikey may be having trouble transitioning from one activity to another, so Arlene began letting Mikey know ahead of time what would happen that day as well as letting him know well in advance of a transition.

But still Mikey struggled.

When Arlene heard about specific praise, she figured it was worth a try. She began to use specific praise with Mikey every step of the getting ready process. "Mikey, you put your sock on your foot!" "Mikey you put your shoes on all by yourself!" "Mikey, I'm so proud of the way you buckled your seat belt without me reminding you!" All of this praise was delivered in a genuinely animated voice punctuated with clapping hands or an amazed "Wow, look at you!" Now, that got Mikey's attention and filled him up with energy as well as self-confidence.

Over time, Mikey began to get ready for the day double quick, and Arlene noticed he was really feeling good about himself. Woohoo!

Okay, so how do I do it?

The trick is to be as descriptive and as animated as you can.
This may feel very weird at first, but as with anything new, the
more you do it, the more natural it will become for you. Being in
a negative pattern for such a long time, it may be very difficult to
notice anything positive at first.

It's important to be positive and genuine. Remember even
acknowledging a fairly neutral behavior will reap benefits. It is
critical to be genuine in your specific praise. Any hint in your
voice that you don't feel truly happy about your child finishing
that one math problem is going to be noted by your child and
heard as criticism.

**Describe exactly what your child is doing in the moment in
clear detail.** If he is using a red crayon, then mention it. If she is
going through those multiplication flash cards really fast then tell
her what you see. The more details the better. This is what
transfers the energy in a positive way.

Notice the process and effort, not just the finished results.
If your child is having particular trouble with certain tasks, then it
is very helpful to energize each step along the way. Don't wait
until the task is completely done or it may never get done!
Remember even small steps towards the goal are worthy of being
acknowledged.

Be animated—GO BIG in how you say praise statements and punctuate them with high fives, hugs, or even joyful laughter to make them even more powerful. Give it a lot of umph!

Do it A LOT, as often as you remember, when you first get started. The more intensely your child seeks energy through negative behaviors, the more specific praise will be needed to shift the balance. Yes, it will be hard at first, but over time it will become easier as your child's behavior becomes more positive.

Avoid "But" Syndrome. "But" Syndrome is adding the word "But" and then making some type of criticism. "I love that you picked up your shirt, but I wish you would keep your room clean all the time." That "But" is like putting a teaspoon of dirt in a clean, refreshing glass of water. Your child will hear "Your room is a mess." Or worse, "You are messy." You would never give a thirsty child dirty water. Don't dirty up your praise with criticism.

Using these tips will help you to praise your child in the most effective way. Remember the more specific praising you do the less yelling and disciplining you will have to do. Yes, really! Your home can be peaceful again.

An example

Here is an example that illustrates a typical situation that my clients report all the time, then the same situation with some specific praise.

Just another day at Sally's house – No specific praise

Sally is playing with blocks on the floor building a tower. Mom sees her and says, "Don't forget to put the blocks away when you are done." Sally frowns and continues to build. She finishes her tower and asks mom to admire it. Mom says, "Oh that's nice. Let's put the blocks in the bucket now if you're done."

Sally puts a couple blocks in the bucket. Mom has turned around to do something else and doesn't notice. Sally wanders off to watch TV. Mom finds the blocks later and yells at Sally for not picking them up. Sally refuses to pick them up which results in her getting a lecture on why it's important to pick up toys when you are finished.

Mom and Sally are both feeling annoyed. Sally got her energy fix from mom, but with a negative pattern. Mom is feeling exhausted and frustrated.

Mom's got a brand new bag – With Specific Praise

Sally is playing with blocks on the floor making a tower. Mom says, "Wow! Sally is making a tall tower out of the blocks!" Sally's behavior is fairly neutral, but her mother is praising her good behavior and feeding her positive energy. Sally feels happy and proud of her tower.

When Sally is done building with the blocks, she puts a few in the bucket. Mom says, "Thank you so much for starting to put away your blocks!" Sally smiles as she finishes putting all the blocks in the bucket. Mom says, "All right Sally!" Gives her a high five. "You put ALL the blocks away! Yeah!"

Sally is clapping for herself, and Mom is smiling happily.

See how different these two scenarios are? It sounds simple, yet these patterns can be very hard to break. It takes a concerted effort by parents to stop the negative spiral and begin setting new positive patterns. The more intense the child has become in seeking negative energy the more energy, mom or dad will need to put into positive behaviors.

I have seen some truly miraculous turnarounds in both child behavior, and also in mom and dad's feelings of well being. It is exhausting to be constantly saying, "Stop!" "No!" "Don't do that!" "I've told you a hundred times. . ." Being a parent is not for the faint of heart, but with a little change, everyone will benefit tremendously.

It works everywhere!

I was a preschool teacher working with 2.5 - 3 year olds in a community center. I had 10 kids in the classroom and some days it seemed impossible to get their attention and distract them from the trouble they were about to get into. I found that by praising them for their good behavior even a split second before they reached for that forbidden item would stop them in their tracks. They would look up and smile at me. It was a joy to see. I began training all my parent helpers in the technique too. The number of timeouts that I gave decreased to none most days. I know many children benefited at home as well!

Examples of ways to phrase specific praise

You picked up two action figures and put them in the bin!

I love the way that you followed my directions the first time!

You shared the Legos with Nick!

I really love the way that you came right away when I called your name.

You did a nice job hanging up your coat and backpack when you came home today.

I like that you used so many colors in your picture! (list the colors)

You are so creative with watercolors.

You are playing so nicely with your sister right now!

You tied your shoes by yourself so fast!

Exclamations add extra energy

Wow!   Fantastic!

That's amazing   Woohoo!

Yeah!   Yes!

That's so cool!

Gestures

Hugs   High fives

Smiles   Thumbs up

Winks   Nodding approval

Patting shoulder, arm, or back

Silly shocked expression

Clapping

Specific Praise Plan Ahead Worksheet

Praise takes a bit a practice, especially if you've been in the negative energy spiral for a while. Thinking now will make it easier to come up with great ideas on the fly. Take some time now to think about how you will construct your praise, then write your answers below:

Starting the praise sentence is often the harder part since the last part of the sentence is more descriptive of what your child is actually doing in that moment. Below write some sentence starters: (I love the way you. . . I am so proud of how you. . . Look how great you are. . ., etc.)

_____

_____

What are some exclamations that you like to use? (Wow! Cool! Way to go! etc.)

_____

_____

What are some gestures that you enjoy using? (Clapping, high fives, etc.)

_____

_____

Get creative with these. The more genuine and heartfelt the more benefits you will enjoy for your child as well as yourself. I'd love to hear what you come up with. Email me and I will post your ideas on my website so that others can be inspired too! http://www.counselingformoms.com/contact.htm

Once you get really good at using specific praise with your child, you may even enjoy trying it out on your husband, your boss, or even yourself!

Go ahead! It's fun!

I have found that specific praise is a simple and highly effective way to improve any child's behavior. As an added bonus, it strengthens your relationship, and also raises your child's self-esteem. It does take some practice and, as with all new ideas, it takes a while to make it a habit. Doing the Specific Praise Challenge described below will help you to start putting the rubber to the road and make specific praise a positive new habit!

Specific Praise Challenge

I have found this technique to be one of the most powerful that I have used both at home with my own kids, in the classroom, and with my client's families. Give it a try for one week.

Go to http://www.counselingformoms.com/specificpraise.htm and fill out the form. A welcome email will be sent to you, click on the link and you will receive helpful tips and reminders each day as well as a worksheet to help you track your progress.

Give your child at least 10 specific praises each day for one week. Then email me at Karen@counselingformoms.com and tell me how it worked out.

Quick Reference: Specific Praise

1. **Be Positive!** By praising even the smallest accomplishment, you are helping your child to feel better about herself and her abilities. Be genuine in your feelings of joy at your child's successes.

2. **Be detailed in your descriptions.** The more specific you are the more powerful the praise. Just saying "good job" or "way to go" is not enough. Make sure your child is very clear about exactly what you are praising them for doing. This is a great way to reinforce your expectations for good behavior.

3. **Notice the process and effort, not just the finished product**. By praising a step towards a final goal, you are helping your child to continue working towards the desired goal. In the case study, Sally was motivated to continue putting the blocks away because Mom praised her for **beginning to put the blocks away.**

4. **Be Animated—GO BIG!** Make your voice sound excited in a genuine way. Use exclamation points with your voice. Punctuate your specific praise with high fives, hugs, and "Woohoo's!" The more energy you put in the more your child will benefit.

5. **Do it often.** If your child is very intense—do it A LOT! Match your child's intensity and need for energy with frequency of specific praise. If your child has problems in a specific area such as homework, be sure to praise every effort no matter how small in the right direction. This will motivate him further to keep going and pick up the pace.

6. **Avoid "But" Syndrome** – Don't add the word "but" onto the ends of your praise statements. For example, "Mikey you did that math problem correctly, but you did it awfully slow." Your child will only hear that he is slow. Ouch!

Behavior as communication

Some of you might remember the detective show called Columbo. (There are episodes on Youtube.com if you want to see them.) As the audience, we always knew who the "bad guy" was, but the fun was in finding out how Lt. Columbo would catch them. He didn't do it with flashy cars or expensive computer systems. He caught them by asking a lot of questions with a calm, curious attitude. The suspects rarely felt defensive, because he was always "just curious." With the information he received, he was able to solve the mystery and catch the murderer.

In my work with clients, I often help problem solve how to change specific challenging behaviors such as refusing to go to bed, melt downs in the grocery store or aggressive behavior with a sibling. Parents tell me that they want to stop these types of behaviors. I have a lot of great techniques and ideas that can work great, yet I find that Columbo's techniques are an important first step. Through calm questioning with a curious attitude, my clients can find out what their child is trying to communicate with that challenging behavior.

Behavior is a type of communication

Children can't always use their words the way that adults do to express themselves. Even many adults are challenged in this area. So, for example, a child might be feeling jealous of a baby sibling and wanting some attention from mom and dad. Chances are you will not hear, "Hey mom, I want attention too!" Instead, you might see your already potty-trained daughter suddenly wetting her pants or your normally generous son grabbing toys out of baby's hands.

Older children may have enough self-awareness to be able to talk to you about why they are doing that annoying behavior, however don't be surprised if you have to do a bit of detective work to get the bottom of it. Here's some keys to help you unlock the mystery just like Columbo:

1. Do it when you and your child are calm.

Talk with your child when you are both calm and comfortable. Columbo usually waited a day or two before questioning a suspect rather than doing it in the heat of the moment. Your child will be much more likely to talk to you about a situation once he has calmed down and gotten some perspective.

2. Have an attitude of respectful, curiosity. This will help to avoid defensiveness which can shut down all communication. Something like this often works: "Hey Johnny, remember yesterday when you got really upset in the grocery store? What was up with that?" This gives the child the opening to explain without feeling judged for the bad behavior. Columbo was a pro at this one.

3. Be patient. It may take more than one conversation to really figure it out. Johnny might say, "Oh, I just hate the grocery store!" Asking more questions might yield that the grocery store is noisier at certain times of the day than others. From there it's easy to problem solve by going shopping during quieter times if you must bring Johnny along. Columbo was always patient and tenacious which was why he was so successful.

Mystery solved

There are some great benefits to knowing what a challenging behavior means before you try to eliminate it including:

- Your child will feel loved, valued and understood.

- You will be able to problem-solve much more effectively since you get to the root of the issue.

- It will be easier for you to remain calm during challenging situations since you will know that your child is trying to communicate something to you, not just trying to drive you insane.

It is not necessary to wear the famous Columbo trench coat and the cigars he smoked are a horrible idea while you solve the mystery of challenging behavior, but that puzzled look works really well!

Expectations Worksheet

The Expectations Worksheet is a tool to use when you have a particular challenging behavior that you want to change. It works really well for very specific problems and helps both adults and children to:

- Understand the problem clearly
- Create an environment that supports the desired behavior
- Reward positive change toward desired behavior
- Give clear consequences for continued problem behavior.

In other words, everyone involved is clear on what the expectations are. It is often surprising to adults that what they thought was straight forward is actually not so obvious to their children. So by talking very explicitly about what is expected and rewarding that behavior, change will begin to happen usually quite rapidly.

One question I get a lot is: "Will I have to do this forever now?" For most problems, you will need to be consistent for a period of time until the desired behavior becomes a habit for your child. Once that happens, then you can use the same system to address another challenge. If you notice that the problem began to reappear, then you can always go back and work the system again. Often, it won't take any time at all to get back on track.

How to get started

First print out a couple of copies of the worksheet. One will serve as a scribbly, draft version, then the other can be re-written a bit neater to be posted some place where everyone can see it.

Next, gather up everyone in the household that is involved with a given problem. If the problem is related to only one child, you may want to involve other children in the family in order make sure that it is fair. For example, if Joe refuses to pick up toys, but Janet picks up without a complaint, then go ahead and involve Janet in the talk. She will find it easy to earn the incentive (we will get to that later) and be a good role model for Joe. Avoid using Janet as an example of model behavior when describing the behavior you want to see or you will be setting yourself up for increased sibling rivalry.

Attitude to bring

As the adult, you will be setting the tone of this discussion, and bringing an attitude of teamwork will go a long ways toward helping your children to cooperate and even enjoy the process. Ask for your child's opinion and advice throughout the process. This will give him a sense of ownership in the plan which will make it much more effective. This should not be arduous, make it fun!

Define the problem behavior

There are two parts to this section The Problem and Desirable Behavior. For each section you want to be specific, concrete, and descriptive. Describe the challenging behavior in detail including what it looks like, when it happens, who does it, how it happens, and where it happens. Then give specific examples. To get the children involved in this process you can ask them to give you examples or even to act out what "NOT" to do. Then do the same thing for Desirable behavior. Give examples and descriptive details as well as time lines. Have the children act out what behavior you want to see.

Write all of this down on your worksheet as you talk about it.

Environmental changes

How can you change the environment to encourage the desirable behavior and discourage the negative behavior?

This is another great question to ask your children. In other words, how can I make it easier for you to do what I want you to do? These changes can be adding things or subtracting things to the environment to make it easier. It could be as simple as adding a larger toy bin or a visual reminder or removing something distracting like turning off the television. Children will often ask for "No yelling" on this item – a win-win for you and for them.

Really get creative here! Remember that you can always come back and make changes if you come up with more ideas at a later time.

Reinforce the desired behavior

Incentive Plans: The five keys to motivation

This is usually the part that children like the best. This is where you and your child get to lay out what reward your child will get for consistently doing the desirable behavior.

Make the goals challenging but reachable. For example, don't expect that your child will be able to do it perfectly at first, but do reward efforts towards the goal, and then slowly over time you can increase the challenge. This is a process after all. Set up your plan to reward good behavior immediately with some type of token. You can use a sticker chart, printable behavior chart, point system, or marbles in a jar. It doesn't really matter as long as you create a system that your child enjoys using and follow the keys for a good system as outlined here.

Finding the reward

There are always lots of things that adults don't want to do—like the dishes, commuting in traffic or paying bills—but we have learned that there are rewards for doing those things and consequences for not doing them. Kids don't always see the big picture the way that we do. They usually don't care if their room is clean or if their homework is done, so it is necessary to create incentives sometimes to help them to understand what is important and what you value as a family.

Creating incentive plans takes quite a bit of creativity, ingenuity, and a bit of "know how." Luckily, the "know how" is fairly easy to explain. Here are the five keys to setting up an incentive plan that really works:

Key #1: Know what kind of child you have

There are two ways that kids want to have incentives. There's the one who wants rewards to be new and different all the time, and the one who consistently likes one type of reward, and it's more satisfying for them and easier for you to just go with that. Granted this can shift and change over time, but by and large most kids will gravitate to one camp or the other.

For example, my son likes only one thing for the most part and that is "screen time"—videogames, portable game systems or computer time is really all he craved. Using a token system wasn't worth the effort because he only wanted to use it for screen time anyway. So, I simplified both of our lives by using 15-minute chunks of screen time as his "token."

One of my client's has a child who wants new and different rewards all the time. His mom created a prize box. She puts in toys from the local dollar store, coupons for special treats or favors, and even quarters for buying gumballs at the grocery store. She also puts in toys that she had to pick up off the floor for him. In other words, if he didn't pick up the toys, he would have to earn it back later. This system keeps the reward always changing and evolving and, boy, does he keep his toys picked up now! Woohoo!

Key #2: Incentive plans should work like the real world

If you ever have a question in your mind about a particular way you want to set up a plan, just think about how incentives work in the real world for grown ups.

A client came to me complaining that the incentive program they were using was not working very well. It was a marble token system where when the child "did something good" he got a marble in the nice, clear jar. When he "did something bad" then a marble would be removed from the jar. When the jar was full then the child would earn some kind of big prize.

Sound reasonable?

Heck no! What happens if ALL the marbles have been removed from the jar? Can you spell Power Struggle? Ugh! Removing a reward that has been earned is a big mistake.

Think about the grown up world. Most people work for money. They do a particular job, and then get paid for that. If you make a mistake in your work, your boss doesn't typically remove money from your paycheck. There is going to be some other type of consequence like a reprimand—or in the worst case a pink slip—but money that you earned is yours period.

Key #3: Use time based incentives as often as possible

Some of the best incentives are what I like to call "time-based" incentives--special times with mom or dad or other important people in your child's life. The beauty of these types of rewards is that they are gone as soon as the reward is "paid." With a prize based reward there is a satiation that happens. "I got the X toy and there's nothing else that I want right now." With time-based rewards they are fleeting, and so easy to renew. You can start a new behavior chart just as soon as you get back from that trip to the local fun park or that bike ride with Grandma. (More on behavior charts in #5)

Key #4: Use your child's love language to inspire your incentives

Finding your child's love language is a really effective way to make incentives that help your child feel loved and valued as well as motivated. Basically the five love languages are as follows:

Acts of Service - helping someone to do errands or chores

Quality Time - One on one, undivided attention

Words of Affirmation - speaking appreciation and acknowledgement

Physical Touch - Hugging, holding hands, massage

Receiving Gifts - receiving objects that show caring and knowledge

By using your child's first or second choice of love language to guide you, you will be able to create a more meaningful as well as motivating incentive.

Key #5: Find fun resources to liven things up a bit

Using a fun behavior chart to track your child's progress can add a lot to the process. Charts don't have to be boring sticker charts. You can make a game out of it. There are some interesting examples that you can use here:

http://www.freebehaviorcharts.com

Of course, if your child IS a big sticker fan then definitely use stickers!

Hopefully, you will find these ideas about incentive systems helpful. Incentives are just one part of a complete parenting plan, but definitely a fun and motivating part. Designing an effective

Parenting plan will allow you to be able to relax and enjoy your child again.

Consequences. What happens if you break the rules?

You probably know by now that you will be asking your child to help you choose this one. While some children will try to find something they can skate through, interestingly, some children who struggle a lot with getting in trouble will come up with some very strict punishments for themselves. You as the adult will need to moderate, so that the "time matches the crime." A consequence can include time outs, loss of privileges, or even extra chores. Creating a logical consequence is best, although not always practical. Be sure that the consequence is something that you can easily enforce if the need should arise. This is not an area for creativity—keep it simple!

A few words about time out.

If you choose to use time out, keep the time short. I have not found that increasing the time helps in anyway. I usually use a 1 or 2 minute timeout which is timed using an egg timer. It is very important to use a timer so that the timer announces when the timeout is over--taking it off your plate. If you are like me, it is easy to get distracted and forget leaving them on timeout longer than necessary and that can lead to defiance in the future. After all, why would you want to get stuck in a time out because your parent got on the phone or something?

Timeout can take place in an out of the way area. Use a stairwell, a corner, or special chair but make sure that it is away from the area of play. Do not talk to the child in timeout; this is not the time for a lecture or a teaching moment. Timeout should be done silently for your child and yourself. Any attention you give in timeout will reward the behavior with energy—don't do it!

As I mentioned before, you won't have to even worry about this very often if you are careful to do all the other steps above it. Timeout is a last resort. When you tell your child to go in time out, use a sad, disappointed voice rather than an angry one. I find that this is very effective in getting them into the time out with a minimum of energy from you.

Consistency is king

It's really important to be consistent with any plan that you set up. That means being consistent with rewards as well as consequences. Often great plans will completely fail if a reward cannot be given in a timely manner. Avoid this at the start by only agreeing to rewards that you can easily provide. For example, if you know that you can't afford a trip to the local amusement park until next month, then set that expectation up at the start, otherwise you will see that the plan will simply not work.

The same goes for consequences. If you set a consequence, you must be willing to enforce it even if that means some sacrifice on your part. Being the "bad guy" sometimes comes with the territory, and you may have to stay home with your child if they didn't earn the reward that other family members received. Chances are good you won't have to do it more than once.

Taking charge

The pay off for setting these firm limits which have been very clearly taught to your child is that your child will for the most part be very comfortable knowing the rules and knowing what to expect from you as well. This actually reduces anxiety in children who are prone to feel like they are in charge of the family.

It is not always easy to stay the course, and if you have had trouble being consistent in the past, then it will be a good idea to have another adult who can back you up when things are starting to slip. Actually, writing out the Expectations Worksheet means, you will be more likely to remember the agreements that you made. Keep them in a special binder that you keep in a spot where it won't get lost—that way you can go back and renegotiate as needed and also refresh your memory about what the heck that reward was anyway.

Another fun way to do this is to set up a plan that the adults in the house also participate in. Dad earns World of Warcraft time and Mom earns a girls night out. This keeps everyone motivated to do those arduous things that they don't enjoy doing. Watching mom and dad do a similar plan is very motivating for kids too.

Give it a try!

For a full page printable version of the Expectations Worksheet, go to:

 http://www.betterbehaviorwithoutstress.com

You'll find resources updates and other helpful information there also.

Expectations Worksheet

1. Define the problem behavior (Be very specific)

The Problem:

Example: Refusing to pick up toys. Leaves toys on the floor or in public areas.

Desirable Behavior:

Example: Picks up toys after one reminder and begins within 30 seconds of being told.

2. Environmental changes. How can you change the environment to encourage the desirable behavior and discourage the negative behavior?

Example: I will buy a toy bin that will be used for toys in the living room.   I will provide a special whisk/dust pan for picking up small pieces.

3. Reinforce the desired behavior. How can you reinforce the behavior you want to see?

Example: I will give specific praise and use a point system for my child to earn a trip to Safari Sam's.

4. Consequences. What happens if you break the rules?

Example: If I pick up toys then they will not be returned until earned back from the prize box.

What to do when nothing is working

If you are consistently applying the techniques above and things are still not going well in a specific area, then it is time to put on your detective hat and figure out from your child where the stumbling blocks are.

Collaborative Problem Solving

Collaborative Problem solving is a very different way of working through problems you have with your child. This process was developed by Ross Greene Ph.D. and described in his book, "The Explosive Child: A New Approach for Understanding and Parenting Easily Frustrated, Chronically Inflexible Children."

Before we discuss the details of this very effective technique, there are a couple of important concepts you need to fully understand and accept. Suspend you disbelief if necessary.

1. Your child is doing the best that he can right now.

This can be hard to swallow at times. You are convinced that your child can and has done better, yet right now he does not appear to be doing at all what you want or expect.

One time my daughter was throwing a grand mal temper tantrum—she was on the floor kicking her feet and screaming bloody murder because I would not allow her to have a fudge pop for breakfast! This was not typical behavior for her at all. I knew that she was well aware that we don't eat dessert for breakfast, yet there we were.

Later, I found out much to my chagrin that she had a very bad ear infection, and her behavior was stemming from that. She was in fact doing the best that she could in the moment, but the best was not what I would want. If I had known about the infection, I probably would have given her more slack than I did. This situation taught me to not make assumptions—I'm still always learning this lesson!

2. Your child is not trying to drive you crazy, manipulate you, or make you upset.

What do I mean by this? You may say to yourself. "No, she knows better than to disobey me." You may say, "He can be sweet and kind, then suddenly for no reason he pinches his sister! How is that doing the best he can?"

Great question! In fact, several possible pieces may be negatively affecting your child's behavior. All children struggle with managing frustration (adults too) but some children, struggle more. Think of it as a frustration tolerance learning disorder. When frustration rises other abilities like speech, impulse control, and social skills go out the window.

So while little Jamey is hitting her little brother, she is in that moment expressing herself. Yes, it's not appropriate expression but acknowledging that she has a reason beyond driving you insane might help you get some perspective on the problem. She has a frustration tolerance learning disability.

If a child has a reading learning disability, you don't punish her for not reading, right? You teach her using a different method than what you tried at first. This is not to suggest that physical aggression doesn't need to have a consequence—it does, but in a different way than how you may have handled it in the past. What I am suggesting is some specialized teaching so that your child can overcome this frustration learning disability.

Collaborative Problem Solving to the rescue!

This is where Collaborative Problem Solving comes in. It uses a specific set of steps that will help you and your child to come up with solution so that bad behavior, meltdowns, and power struggles can become a thing of the past. If this sounds too good to be true, let me assure you that it does require practice and effort on both yours and your child's part.

Okay, think about having three plans of action whenever there is a problem. The three plans are:

Plan A – Enforcing your will (what you are doing now)

Plan C - Just let it go for now (what you do when you are too tired to fight now)

Plan B - Collaborative Problem Solving

Let's look at the plans in detail.

Well, Plan A has got you nothing but exhausted up until now. Sure, it works sometimes, but it also exacts a price in terms of power struggles, meltdowns, and painful relationships.

Plan C is just letting it go for now. This plan is not as bad as it sounds as long as you do it consciously. You can't work on every problem at the same time. By prioritizing what is most important first then working down the list, eventually you will reach your goals. Think of Plan C as picking your battles, so that you can focus on what is most important.

The worst combination is when you start to do Plan A, then get exhausted and resort to Plan C to try to pacify the situation. This teaches your child that melting down gets her what she wants. She soon learns that you will give up if she pushes you hard enough. Even if you only do this a few times, this pattern can get put in place very quickly and be hard to undo.

Okay, so how does Plan B Collaborative Problem Solving work?

Plan B involves three steps

1. Empathy
2. Defining the problem
3. Invitation

Let's look at these steps in order.

Step 1: Empathy

Empathy is the first step because it keeps people calm. When you feel heard and understood, you are less likely to go into a melt down. Once a melt down is happening, there is no point in trying to do Plan B, just wait it out then when things are calm again you can use Plan B. If you can get the empathy going quickly enough, you may be able to stop the melt down before it occurs. This takes some practice, so if you don't do it perfectly the first time, don't worry. You will get it.

Empathy needs to be kept simple and direct. The most effective way is to simply re-state what your child says, then ask the question, 'What's up with that?" For example, Johnny is refusing to pick up his Legos.

Johnny: "No I won't pickup!"

Mom: "You won't pick up the Legos. What's up with that?"

At this point Johnny will probably say more about why he is refusing, and then Mom can further refine her empathy.

Johnny: "I don't want to go to bed yet!"

Mom: "Oh you don't want to pick up the Legos because you don't want to go to bed now."

Johnny: "I'm not sleepy yet!"

Mom: "You don't want to pick up the Legos because you are worried about going to bed and you are not sleepy yet?

Johnny: Yes!

Step 2: Define the Problem

This is where the adult gets to express her concern. A problem is when there are two concerns on the table—yours and your child's. It's important to remember that you are expressing a CONCERN here not your solution. If a solution is on the table then you are using Plan A.

Mom: I understand that you are not sleepy now and you're worried about going to bed right away. I'm not saying that you have to go to bed right away. I'm concerned that if we don't pick up the Legos that they could be stepped on and broken or lost.

Step 3: The invitation

Here you will invite your child to help you solve the problem. A good solution considers both concerns and is doable and realistic. This does not mean that Johnny is now responsible for coming up with a solution—only that you are inviting him to try to come up with an agreeable solution. This is a process of learning, so your child will probably need help at first. If your child is like most, he will probably surprise you, but maybe not at first.

Mom: Do you have any ideas?

Johnny: "I'm not picking up."

This is a good sign that Johnny still has some learning to do about solutions. Don't tell him that this is a "bad solution" or you may end up with a melt down. Instead, remind him that both concerns must be addressed, then repeat both concerns, and ask "Any ideas?"

If he says, "No." then it will be a good time to ask if he would like help to think of something.

Mom: How about we pick up the Legos together, then we can read two books before going to get ready for bed?

Johnny: No, I don't want to pick up!

Mom: Well, what other ideas do you have? (mom stays quiet to give Johnny a chance to add something)

Johnny: I don't know. . .

Mom: Hmmm

Johnny: Okay, I'll pick up these and you pick up those. . .(starts picking up Legos)

Mom: Sounds like a plan, let's do it!

If Johnny is used to Plan A being used all the time, it may take him a while to get used to going Plan B. He may even get pretty heated up. This process will take some getting used to.

Two types of Plan B

There are two types of Plan B.

Emergency Plan B – A Pre-emptive strike before a melt down

Pro-Active Plan B -- Taking a known trigger and working on it before it becomes a problem again.

Emergency Plan B is used to attempt to way lay a melt down. Through using the Empathy step, you may be able to calm the child down enough to begin using his rational thinking skills again. Then proceed through the problem solving steps. Chances are that solutions found in an emergency will need to be re-visited pro-actively later.

Pro-Active Plan B is used to prevent a problem from occurring again in the future. By identifying triggers that cause problems, you will be able to start a Plan B conversation before a situation arises again. By having the conversations when things are calm, you will be able to arrive at good, lasting solutions that avoid those triggers and thus avoid power struggles and melt downs.

Misconceptions about Plan B

Many parents worry that doing Plan B will somehow be giving up their authority as a parent. Nothing could be further from the truth. In fact, your concerns as the adult are on the table as well. By allowing your child to participate in Problem Solving you are teaching them a skill that they will use everyday of their lives.

Plan B is not a magic bullet. It's hard work and sometimes the first solution you decide on doesn't work. Try try again. It may take several problem-solving discussions to find lasting solutions to very difficult problems. It takes practice and persistence to give up Plan A. After all, isn't that the way we were parented? The fact is that Plan A doesn't work with our easily frustrated child, but with effort, Plan B can make a huge difference.

How am I supposed to stay calm?

Pretty much all of the parenting techniques in this book hinge on one very important and very difficult concept for parents:

Staying Calm!

So when your child is getting on your very last nerve and your old way of handling it might have been a very loud tirade—who am I to ask you to stay calm?

What happened to me

I am a mom like you who was really struggling and at times I still struggle to keep from losing it. I will never forget one time I was trying a new technique with my son, and he decided to retaliate by peeing on the floor of his bedroom.

Did I stay calm?

Uh. . .not so much.

I completely lost it and called the psychologist who recommended the technique. Crying, I explained what I did and then what my son did and asked him tearfully what I'm supposed to do now. He asked me if I had any friends that I could talk to.

Needless to say, I never went back to that person again. I also don't recommend that technique I was trying that day. Guess what? It's a recipe for power struggles and escalation, which is exactly what I was trying to stop at the time.

However, as offended as I was at the time, in fact, I did desperately need some friend time. I was exhausted from not sleeping and completely overcome with guilt that I was to blame for my son having so much trouble. I was a single mom working full time and grieving over a recent divorce.

So if you think that I don't know how hard this is—please know that I really have been there, and I really do know how hard it can be to keep yourself calm amidst the chaos in your home.

I also know very well how powerful it will be when you are able to stay calm. How it helps your child to calm down sooner, and how much better you will feel about your abilities as a parent. I know because I have experienced that side of it also, and you can too.

So how are you supposed to pull this off? I have two words for you:

Self care

You spend all day taking care of other people--your kids, your partner, your friends, and your boss. How much time do you devote to yourself? I'm going to guess that number is very small. You have probably heard that metaphor about putting on your own oxygen mask before putting on your child's oxygen mask in an airplane?

I think that while we get that idea intellectually—emotionally it's going right past us. I include myself in this one too. I believe that most of us are taught as young children that we can "have it all" if we work hard enough and smart enough. So we work hard and hope we are smart, and then hope somehow we will have the perfect family, perfect relationship, and perfect career, etc. etc. I think if we really look at some of these beliefs and actually think about what perfect means, that we might begin to live our lives differently.

Looking at your beliefs about self care

Getting clear about your beliefs around self care and then challenging those beliefs that make it hard for you to actually do those things that are nourishing to you, is a great way to get started. Spend some time with the questions below. Talk over your answers with a supportive friend, family member, or therapist.

When I think about taking time just for myself, I feel:

I expect that if other people know I needed time just for myself, they would think:

I notice when I take time for myself that my loved ones are:

Some things that get in the way of me setting aside time for myself are:

If I were to let go of those things that get in my way, I would:

Make a list of all the ways that you do self care now:

Make a list of other self care activities that you wish you could do more of:

Some Self-Care ideas

Basically, self-care is any activity that nourishes you--body, mind and soul. Below is a list of some ideas for self-care for each of these three areas. Use this list for your own inspiration. You are the best judge of what is nurturing to you.

Body

- Getting an appropriate amount of sleep each night in order to feel refreshed and rested (7-8 hours for most people)
- Eating a healthy, well balance meal slowly and mindfully.
- Doing a fun physical activity like
    - Dancing to a favorite song
    - Playing tennis with a friend
    - Going for a nature hike
    - Taking a stroll around the neighborhood
- Taking a bubble bath
- Lighting a scented candle
- Looking at some beautiful photography, art, or scenery
- Watching a film that you love
- Listening to music that help you feel relaxed or energized as the mood strikes you.

Mind

- Going out with a friend for coffee or a meal
- Talking on the phone with a friend
- Journaling or creating some kind of expressive art project
- Counseling
- Learning something new
- Reading something fun inspiring, or informative

Soul

- Spiritual Practice – prayer, meditation
- Attending services or study groups
- Reading or listening to inspiration materials
- Taking a class or workshop on a topic related to your faith

Making self care a priority in your life

Obviously, there is a lot of overlap between the categories for example a nature hike could be spiritually as well as physically satisfying for me. So don't worry about where it fits, but rather prioritize the highly nurturing experiences over the less nurturing experiences. Create a list for yourself of all the nurturing activities that you do now, that you have done in the past and that you would love to do, but "never have the time" to do.

Now pull out your calendar, Day-Timer, or PDA and schedule yourself some time each week. Try scheduling at least an hour each week. You can spread it out over several days or take it all in a lump.

New habits take persistence

I understand that if you have not already been doing this, it may take some persistence at first. You may find yourself blowing through it to take care of someone else, or you may find that your family members or others in your life are not on board yet.

It takes times to build up new habits, but the efforts that you put into nurturing yourself will pay big dividends later in better health, better moods, and more calmness.

You will notice yourself being:

- More patient
- More positive
- Better able to problem solve
- More confident in your own abilities

And guess what? This is a big piece of what you need to begin calming the chaos in your home. Yes, really! So as odd as it may feel at first increasing your self-care is the first step towards helping your family and yourself to be happier and more successful.

Dealing with specific situations

In this section I will discuss specific problems that I hear about constantly from clients, from parent support group members, or just reading parenting blogs and forums on the Internet. Some of these you will recognize from my Calm The Chaos newsletter and others will be brand new topics. I hope that these extended examples will explain in more detail some ways to apply the basic tools described previously to specific problems that you might be dealing with every day.

Transitions: How to avoid meltdowns

Struggling with transitions is something that seems to affect most of our kids. Actually, it affects most of us too if we think about it.

Our family went camping one time. We had great weather the whole time until the last night. Yep, it started to rain in August! I normally love our Pacific Northwest rain, but this sudden unexpected transition really threw me. The whining and complaining wasn't coming from the kids that night! I recovered quickly enough, and our equipment dried nicely in the garage. <sigh>

Transitioning from one activity to another is very difficult for most kids and for some, it can trigger meltdowns and power struggles. Leaving the activity they are engaged in now to begin another task, no matter how pleasurable is extremely hard to do. If the new activity is less pleasurable, then just forget it. Meltdown city!

Here are a few tips to help:

1. **Daily overviews** – give your child an overview of the basic schedule for the day. If you have a highly visual child then make this a visual schedule with pictures. This is especially helpful for major changes like when school starts.

2. **Warnings** – As a transition time is nearing give several warnings that it's almost time to transition. For example, to transition from the playground to home for lunch. Call out a 10 minute warning, a 5 minute warning and a 1 minute warning. Be sure to praise your child for coming when time is up.

3. **Using a timer** can also be helpful for older children who don't like "being nagged." A regular kitchen timer will work great. This takes you out of the picture and puts it with your child. When the

timer goes off, he knows what it means and what he is to do next. This expectation needs to be very clear.

4. **Specific Praise** – Make an effort to praise your child's efforts toward transitioning. "Wow, look how many blocks you picked up! High five buddy!" This will go a long way toward energizing your child's efforts no matter how small they may seem at first.

5. **Re-evaluate** – While having a structured day is important—having enough downtime is also important. Flexibility towards your child's needs in the moment can make a big difference in your child's behavior and your sanity. For example, if you notice that afternoons are more stressful, then maybe lowering the number of activities in the afternoon will help. Figuring out what the triggers are can really make a big difference.

Transitions become easier with time and practice, but some children continue to struggle long after their peers and even younger siblings. Try these techniques and things will start to improve right away.

Social Skills: Embarrassing moments

My son and I are standing in line at the grocery store. There is a fairly large, attractive black woman standing in front of us in the line. My beloved boy takes one look and says, "Oh. My. God. Look at how HUGE that woman's. . ." I put my hand firmly on his mouth at that point! Oy! I was so embarrassed! I must have turned six shades of purple. I explained to him for the 876,000th time that we don't talk about other people's body parts. I have a dream that some day he will actually understand, but that is still a work in progress.

I think most every parent at one time or another has been embarrassed by something your child did in public. If your child struggles more than others with a deficit in social skills like mine, then this may be an everyday experience. I think it can be easy to get used to our children's quirks at home, but out in the world that brutal honesty might get him a dirty look or worse a punch in the nose, that constant chatter about her special interest might get her shunned by peers, and that bossy attitude might land him in the Principal's office—again.

Why does he do this stuff anyway?

Sure a diagnosis of ADHD, high functioning autism, Asperger's Syndrome, etc. explains that there is a social skills deficit, but is it possible to teach something that most people learn intuitively?

The answer is yes!

Social skills can be taught just like any other set of skills since they don't come naturally, each skill must be specifically taught, and not only how to do a skill, but when and why need to taught as well. Here are three keys to beginning to help your child improve his or her social skills.

Three Keys to Better Social Skills

1. **Self Awareness** – Helping your child to become more aware of how his or her behavior affects others. You can do this by becoming a mirror for your child. You can do this as a game or by using a video camera to build awareness of how he is perceived.

2. **Other Awareness** – stop the action on his or her favorite video and ask how a particular character might be feeling inside right now or what reasons they might have for how they are acting right now. If your child is not able to make accurate guesses about these things at first, be careful to not make him wrong, but matter of factly explain what you see.

3. **Situational Awareness** – When you notice a particular social challenge arising within your family, stop the action and start a discussion about what is happening at that moment. For example, if your child is going on and on about his special interest, but the other family members are no longer listening. Stop the action and ask your child to notice the people around him right now. How are they holding their bodies, what expression is on their faces, etc.? Have him or her guess how the other people might be reacting to his or her behavior in the moment.

By building awareness, your child will begin the process of noticing and thinking about how he or she feels as well as how other people are affected by his behaviors.

Social Skills: Teach it don't knock it

No trash talk for grandpa

I was talking to my husband about a new social skills topic, and I explained to him that children who struggle with social skills often don't understand that some behaviors are okay with some people and at some times, but not okay with other people or at other times. For example, arm farts are really funny and very acceptable when you are with your other 3rd grade friends on the playground or hanging around outside at home, but those same very funny arm farts will get you a trip to the principals office if you do it in the classroom or a time out if you do it at Grandma's house.

"Aaah." Said my husband with that dreamy look in his eye that tells me that he is remembering his own past arm fart fun. Suddenly he said, "So how do you teach that?" "Well," I said off handedly, "You just talk about it. Most of the time we just tell them to "Knock it off" and that's it. We assume that they know that this is not the right time. In fact, most of the time they must get pretty confused because they really don't understand when it is okay and when it is not."

I didn't think anymore about it that day, but the next day my husband happily told me a story about putting this little idea of mine on the road.

Taking the idea on the road

We were at an art fair with our extended family. My dad's hip was bothering him, so I walked him back to the car, and my son was tagging along. When we arrived my husband was already at the car, so he took both of them back to the house. My typically stoic dad was telling my husband about how much pain he is in when my son pipes up from the backseat, "Oh yeah, you think that's bad, you should have felt how much pain, I was in last week!"

My husband immediately recognized that my son was acting in an inappropriate manner—some would even say that he lacked empathy—but rather than just tell him to "Knock it off." He explained to my son that talking like that would be okay with his buddies.

(Imagine for a moment: a group of boys standing in a circle comparing war wounds. "Oh yeah, when I cut my arm it bled for an hour!" "Oh yeah, when I broke my arm the bone was sticking out!" "Oh yeah. . .")

My husband also explained that this is not an appropriate way to talk to Grandpa when he is in pain. My husband said that he saw that little light bulb go off over my son's head that day.

The other added benefit was that this conversation also helped my dad to better understand my son's social skills challenges.

Sibling combat: Let's call a truce!

Family time is traditionally a time of backyard barbeques, playing board games together, snuggling up with a good movie, and . . .

beating up your pesty little brother.

Okay okay, not exactly your idea of an ideal family pastime? Mine either! Yet, unstructured play times and family vacations often mean more brothers and sisters are stuck playing together. More togetherness often means more chances for conflict.

This is how it works in many homes:

Sister says something rude to brother.
Brother gets infuriated then smacks sister.
Sister cries and brother gets in trouble.

That's not fair!

While hitting is the more serious offense, the fact is that sister also did something. By not giving her a consequence, you are unwittingly reinforcing her behavior, which will continue to instigate his behavior. Since an adult is not always around to know the details of what exactly happened, I suggest always giving a consequence to both combatants, I mean, children. . .

This does several things:

- It stops siblings from endlessly picking on each other in order to get the more impulsive child in trouble.

- It builds teamwork thinking in the children. Since they know they will both get in trouble, they are less likely to "tattletale" on each other for every little thing.

- It is fair. It takes two to tango and also to fight. Innocent victims are rare in this scenario.

Obviously, there are exceptions to this rule, but by and large, it works and helps to lower the amount of sibling fighting that goes on.

Working it out

In order to help kids work through or avoid conflict, it's important to teach them how to handle it themselves. The tendency to step in and separate the combatants just to return to peace is overwhelming, but allowing them to work through their conflicts together can yield big rewards in the long run. Follow these steps to restore peace:

- Stop the physical fighting or the yelling and request that both parties use a calm voice.
- Give each sibling a chance to tell their side of the story without interruptions from the other.
- Ask clarifying questions until you feel that all the important details about the disagreement are on the table.
- Help them to summarize their concerns and get agreement that you understand everything.
- Ask them to both come up with solutions that address both concerns as well as your concern about the fighting.
- If they need help coming up with solutions that address both concerns, then give them some ideas.
- Take a deep breath to keep yourself calm too. Your children are going to calm down faster if you are calm.

This process of collaborative problem solving is not easy for kids to do at first. It does take practice, but it is a skill that will serve them the rest of their lives.

Motivation to do chores

I have heard from many parents over the years asking about how to motivate a child to do things they don't want to do. Chores, homework, and even specialized classes were mentioned. It's an interesting question. Nobody really loves to clean the bathroom do they? Okay, you two who do love it—just go with me here for a moment. :) Not to mention who loves nagging others to do those things?

Here are some ideas that you can use to help make unpleasant tasks a little less arduous for your child. The extra bonus is that it requires no nagging from you. I'll be using cleaning a bedroom as an example, but the basic ideas can be used for just about anything.

- Clear instructions to avoid overwhelm.
- Break task up into smaller bites.
- Set up the environment for success.
- Praise all efforts.
- Add an incentive for a job well done.

Clear Instructions to avoid overwhelm

This may sound odd. Of course, your child knows how to clean his room! In fact, many children get overwhelmed with too many instructions at once or with instructions that are too general. "Go clean your room" actually means something like this:

- "Go pick up all your dirty clothes and put them in the hamper, and then pick up all the Legos and put them in the bucket, and then pick up all the action figures and put them in the bin, and then pull the covers up on the bed, and then pick up all the stuffed animals and arrange them on your bed, and then pick up all the tiny pieces of toys, beads, paper, what have you and put them away or throw them away, and then go through your dresser and pull out all the clothes you don't wear anymore and put them in the Goodwill box, etc. etc."

You would never give someone this many instructions to do at once, and yet that simple statement "Go clean your room." sounds like this to your child. It's overwhelming. What do children who are overwhelmed do?

- They refuse to do the task.
- They put it off until later.
- They try to distract you into forgetting about it.

Breaking the task up into smaller bites

To avoid overwhelm, give your child one very specific instruction at a time.

- "Go pick up 10 articles of dirty clothes and put them in the hamper." "Go pick up 20 action figures and put them in the bin."

You can adjust the number of items to the age and ability of the child. (and discover how many figures there actually are!) An older child may be able to take in larger chunks, while a younger child will need even smaller pieces.

Setup the environment for success

This may not be so obvious to you, but it makes a huge difference. Make sure that the environment is set up to allow your child to easily finish the task at hand. Some things to think about might be:

- Is there a properly sized bin or other container for all items to be put away?
- Are there tools available to help out (such as

brush/dust pan for getting all those beads out of the carpet)
- Is the trashcan, Goodwill box, and hamper in the room so they are not walking around the house where distractions are more likely?
- Are you available to continue giving directions and praising efforts?

Praise all efforts

You knew I was going to say this. Once they have completed a task successfully, praise them, "Wow, you picked up 10 items! The room looks better already. Let's do some more!" (Given with a high five or a hug)

Then you can give the next instruction. It's a good idea to have the first few instructions make a big difference in the room, so that they can see how quickly they are making progress. Don't skip this praise step it is CRUCIAL. They will get a lot more motivated by your excitement about their progress than about seeing the room look cleaner.

Add an incentive for a job well done

Some may have a problem with this step. After all you shouldn't bribe your child to do chores right? Well, if you think about it, incentives are used all the time in our society and as long as you follow the basic rules for incentives, I think they are not only very appropriate, but very effective.

Okay, now go get those bedrooms sparkling!

Back talk

Many parents have identified back talk by their children as one of their most difficult parenting challenges. After all, when your child back talks you isn't your first urge to give it right back? Yet, this urge is actually counterproductive because you are modeling the very same bad behavior you want them to stop doing.
Doesn't work so well. . .

So what's a mom or dad to do? Well, let's look under the hood and see what is underneath that snotty remark. Those bratty remarks and obnoxious comments are actually covering up some other concern. For example, your child might be feeling overwhelmed by what you just asked him to do, but rather than say that, he spouts off with back talk.

So the trick is to address the underlying feeling rather than the angry words. By ignoring the obnoxious remarks, you are not giving that behavior any of your energy. Also, you are not modeling that same anger back which does nothing to address the real problem. This anger is a distraction from the real underlying issue and by addressing that you get what you want and your child's concerns are addressed—win/win.

So instead of yelling back, you tilt your head to the side in a quizzical expression and ask calmly "What's got you so upset?" or some other open ended general question. Your child will respond. Repeat the words your child says in the form of a question, then wait for more information. Continue doing this until you get down to the real issue at hand.

Here is an example of how it might work:

Mom: Joanie, go clean your room!

Joanie: Forget it! I'm not doing it!

Mom: What's up with that? (Voice is calm, expression questioning)

Joanie: You are so mean to me all the time!

Mom: I'm so mean to you all the time? (again calm, questioning)

Joanie: You are always getting on my case!

Mom: I'm on always on your case? I just asked you to clean your room? (notice how Mom doesn't engage that and brings things back to the current situation which is the room cleaning)

Joanie: It's too much to do! (Ah, now we have the turning point—a sign of overwhelm)

Mom: Oh, it seems like too much to do and maybe you are feeling overwhelmed?

Joanie: Yeah, just look at it! I don't know where to start!

Now Mom knows that Joanie is overwhelmed by the idea of cleaning her room and doesn't know where to get started. Mom can help Joanie to break the project up into smaller steps so that it doesn't seem so overwhelming. Joanie is calmer now because her concerns are being addressed. Mom never lost her cool, and the room is getting cleaned. Everybody wins.

Now you may ask how does the actual back talk get addressed? By not acknowledging the anger and instead addressing the real concern, you are modeling good communication skills to your child. Over time, your child will begin expressing their feelings more directly, but this is a skill that comes with practice over time.

Difficult Mornings: Setting up Expectations

Many families struggle in the morning. There are many specific things that must be completed within a specific timeframe in order for parents to get to work on time and children to get to school on time. This means that there is less room for negotiation than there might be at other times.

To add to the stress of these time constraints this is the time of day that is often the most difficult for many of us to be at our best.

We are still tired.

We might be dreading the day ahead.

Our medications may not be working yet.

We may be feeling fuzzy headed which makes it harder to get even the most simple things accomplished.

We may be eating when we are not hungry yet.

All of these things create a perfect storm of stress that often ends with parents yelling and frustrated and kids crying and angry. Not the best way to start the day!

Expectations Worksheet to the rescue!

This situation is the perfect opportunity to set up a really clear behavior plan. By clarifying exactly what you want to see and what you do not want to see in the mornings, your child will be able to get into a routine that will make things less stressful for both of you. By creating a good incentive for this you will find that your child will be that much more motivated to do what needs to be done without a lot of push back.

Call a meeting of the minds

The first step is to print out the form and call a family meeting. Talk over the problems that everyone sees in the morning. Invite the kids to talk about what they don't like about the mornings as well. The things that they say may surprise you. Take some deep breaths and try not to react defensively to this feedback. These are the reasons your kids will be motivated to try this new system and make it work! Now write out very specifically the behaviors that you do not want to see. Some of these might be: refusing to get up on time, dawdling over breakfast, playing, watching tv or doing other activities before completing everything that has to be done. Write all of these out.

Defining the desirable behavior

The first step is to have the family talk about what types of behaviors you do want to see in the morning. You may want to write out a schedule with times or draw pictures in the order that the routine is to be completed. Wake up, get dressed, brush hair, eat breakfast, brush teeth, put on jacket, put on backpack, go to the bus stop. You get the idea. This needs to be as specific and clear as you can make it. The idea is to make it easy for your kids to follow. It is important to gear these changes to your child's abilities and developmental level. Your three year old will have a much simpler routine than your 12 year old for example, but the process to get there is the same. If you have concerns that your child may not be able to do it, then try creating a simpler system then adding the more difficult pieces after the new routine has become very easy for your child to do.

Setting up the environment for success

Now have everyone put their heads together to think of ways to make it easier to do what is expected and less likely to do the problem behaviors. Some ideas might be: set out clothes the night before, put all homework and important papers into the backpack the night before, keep TV and radios off, and talk over what breakfast food is preferred.

This part of the conversation is very important and more you are able to make things easier the more likely that things will go smoother in the morning. Remember this is always a work in progress so as new problems crop up, you can always come back and create new ways to make things easier.

Reinforcement: Woohoo you did it!

This is where you get to set a reward for when the desired behavior has happened a certain number of times. Definitely have the kids come up with some ideas for rewards. I would highly recommend an event based reward if you can because that way as soon as you go do the activity, the hunger to do it again is there. With physical rewards like games or other toys, there is a satiation that happens which might make the old behaviors start to creep up again.

It is very important that the reward matches the amount of effort involved and is mutually agreeable. If you have any doubt about being able to pull off a reward, then pick something else. A child who earns a reward and then gets disappointed is a child who will likely not participate in the future. It's just not worth it!

Consequences: Breaking the rules

As with rewards, it is important that your kids have a say in what consequences are if the problem behavior happens rather than the desirable behavior. You need to be very specific about what would have to happen to create the consequence as well as what the consequence might be. For example for missing the bus, the child would have to do a specific chore when they get home from school. After all, you had to take time out to drive them to school its only fair that they pay you back with their time doing a chore. I find that if the first three steps are carried out faithfully then you will almost never have to actually have a consequence.

Working the system

Use specific praise statements to reinforce efforts in the right direction especially right in the beginning, that way your child will know he is on the right track and keep working hard to earn that cool reward. You can use a sticker chart, a point system or any of the many very cool systems on the market to track success. This doesn't need to be anything fancy to be really helpful.

Not turning in homework

Many of our kids have a very hard time remembering to turn in homework, even though they may have slaved for hours on it the night before! This is frustrating to parents, teachers and children. There are several ideas that may work, but since so many children seem to be very visually oriented having a visual reminder can be very helpful. Sit with your child and look at the binder system that he is using at school now. When he sits down in the classroom what is the first thing that he does? The second thing? By analyzing your child's behaviors you can build in a reminder into the behaviors that are already happening.

For example, lets say that when my son arrives to his math class he will pull his math book and his math notebook out of his backpack. Then he will open his binder to the current page. What if you put a clear plastic envelope with the homework in it in that spot in the binder? The homework will literally act as its own reminder. This is another way to set up the environment to make it easier for your child to do what you want him to do.

Can't sleep again?

Sleep problems are one of those challenges that not only are hard on children and those who care for them at night, but that constant exhaustion during the day seems to make even the most simple tasks that much harder. Whether it is because of problems with transitions, sensory issues, or an over active mind that is racing fifty thousand miles an hour, one thing is abundantly clear, and that is that a child who is not getting enough sleep is going to have a harder time coping with frustration, managing emotions, and often will be more hyperactive physically. A sleep deprived child (or adult for that matter) will have a harder time learning because it is in sleep when our brains transfer information from short term memory into long term memory.

So, I know I don't need to convince you or anyone else how important good quality sleep actually is. Yet, it seems to be quite elusive at times. None of my children sleep well, but two of them have very difficult problems with sleep. Here is a bit about our family's sleep challenges and what we did.

War Zone at Bedtime

Every night my son would start getting hyper right before bed and throw grand mal temper tantrums complete with destruction of his own beloved toys and kicks aimed directly at my shins. I pretty much had permanent bruises on my shins from the time he turned age 2 until age 9.

There were many theories over the years for my son's difficulties at bedtime.

"He's too stimulated by the TV or video games or rough housing too close to bedtime?"

"He's having trouble transitioning from wakefulness to sleep."

"He is struggling with anxiety."

"He is trying to drive me insane, and it's working!"

You can probably guess which one was my theory at the time. I was getting pretty desperate. His lack of sleep was affecting his ability to manage his emotions, so this became a downward spiral with more and more severe temper tantrums during the day and continuing at bedtime.

My own sleep was also being affected, so that was not helping matters either. To add to the stress, his dad and I were also having disagreements about the best way to handle this with each of us pointing at the other.

What we tried

I took my son to a psychologist and began using Behavior Modification techniques. It helped him to control how much damage he was doing, but he was still having a hard time getting to sleep. Things were enough better that I was willing to cope for a while, but he was still struggling during the day with sleepiness and irritability due to lack of sleep. Poor little guy had dark circles under his eyes!

I began to study sleep in earnest. What helps and what doesn't, but all the books were either about babies (cry it out?? yuck) or about adult insomnia remedies many of which were just not going to work for a little boy. I tried guided imagery and soothing music, but he just couldn't cooperate when he was so tired.

Finally, I took him to his primary care provider again and talked to her about the sleep problem. By now my son was 9 years old, and there were other things that interested her, and she asked a lot of questions about his habits, behaviors, social skills, etc. Then she provided us with a referral to a pediatric neurologist who did thorough assessment, and then referred us to a psychiatrist who prescribed a medication.

This was a huge step for us. I was not very happy at the prospect of giving my son medications that had not been properly studied for children even though I had plenty of people saying that this particular one helped their children tremendously. My son actually got worse—much worse. He was going to sleep easily, but having nightmares. We had taken two giant steps backwards, and he was getting kicked out of school almost daily and becoming increasingly aggressive at home as well. This was a giant step backwards.

We took him back to the psychiatrist who then took him off that medication and put him on a different one which was actually a blood pressure medication oddly enough. Now he was able to go to sleep easily and sleeping well for the first time in his life it seemed like. He started having good days again. He was able to manage his frustrations easier too. I was sold that this was a miracle drug.

Eventually, however, my son's father decided that since he is doing so well that we should take him off his medication. I was mad at first. It made no sense to me to take him off if he is doing so well on them. But his dad insisted so that is what we did.

In the meantime, I went to a naturopathic physician who gave me a homeopathic remedy called Pulsatilla. Homeopathic remedies are small white pills that melt in your mouth and provide tiny amounts of some type of substance for various ailments. Pulsatilla is billed as being for yellow mucus on the package (I know weird huh?), however, I have found that it works very well for relaxation. I found that sometimes when I am feeling kind of raw and over stimulated myself, this works amazing for that . . . I have no clue about how that relates to yellow mucus, but don't let it hold you back. This is a very nice way to take the rough edges off.

I found that my son also does well with it and will mellow out within a couple of minutes of taking it with absolutely no side effects or concerns about side effects. He will refuse to take it sometimes now saying that he doesn't need anything, but when he does, it works quite well even by his own admission. Talk to your naturopathic physician about what might be a good option for your child.

Then one of my daughter's began to have sleep problems. In the Summer months she would flip over to overnight shift hours. Wakeful at night and sleeping in the day time. She was looking exhausted all the time. So we started trying natural remedies. The Pulsatilla did nothing for her. We tried sleepy time tea, Valerian Root, 5HTP, Benadryl, and lastly Melatonin. Only the Melatonin seemed to make a difference for her. She was able to fall asleep with it and stay asleep.

I would highly recommend checking in with a naturopathic physician or medical doctor before trying out herbal or homeopathic remedies. There are many good options out there, and it helps to have an expert who can direct you on dosages and any interactions with other prescriptions. Everyone's brain chemistry is so different so what works for one will not necessarily work for another—experiment and see what works best for you and yours.

Sensory Visualization

While this technique did not work for my son, I do find that it works well for me and for many of my clients. It is basically a three-step process:

- Slow deep breathing
- Remind yourself that it is time for resting
- Visualize some place calming and relaxing using all your senses.

Let's take one at a time and go into more detail. This technique requires some practice, so don't be surprised if you are not able to do it perfectly the first time. Keep practicing, and you will be able to relax and take a mini vacation whenever you need one.

Breathing

Proper breathing is highly effective in relaxing the body and calming the mind. It is very simple, yet many of us do it incorrectly. In order to get the full benefit of deep breathing follow these steps.

- Put your hand on your belly and breath in until your

hand moves.

- Breathe in to the count of 4, hold your breathe to the count of 4 then breathe out to the count of four. You can adjust that number if 4 is not comfortable. Smokers may need to use the count of 3 while people with more lung capacity can use 5 or 6. Start with 4 and then play around and see what works best for you.
- Once you have a good rhythm, you can stop counting and move on to the next steps.

Right thinking

It seems like late at night is a good time to stress out over the details of the day. Whether it is "I should have said. . ." or "What did that mean when they. . ." or any other combination of stressful thoughts about the day before or stressing about the future like: "I can't forget that I need to. . ." or "I just know I'm going to screw up. . ." You get the idea. Our brains can work over time creating all kinds of drama and anxiety when we are trying to relax and get some rest. The key is to challenge those stressful thoughts and remind yourself that now is the time to rest and not stress.

Is that true?

One way to challenge stressful thoughts is to ask yourself, "Is that true?" and try to look at the situation objectively. Often, there may be a grain of truth there, but you are going overboard in some way. For example, your child may be worried about flunking a test. Reminding your child that he is good at that subject or that he has never flunked before may help to relieve his mind somewhat. Obviously, this tactic will not work if the worrisome thing is actually truly something to be worried about.

Can I do anything about this now?

When the worrisome thoughts are actually true worries then reminding your child that there is nothing to be done about it right now, but tomorrow there are things that can be done. So if he is worried about flunking a test because he did not study, then reminding him that now would not be a good time to study, but that he can get up in the morning and study a bit before the test. Obviously, a long lecture would not be helpful here either.

Now is time to rest – mind and body

Simply, having your child repeat the phrase. "Now is time for resting." Can be very helpful to reset the brain from spinning to, well, resting. If your child seems to be physically agitated or hyperactive, it can be helpful to have them lay in bed and isolate particular body parts then tense the muscles and release them. For example, tense up your feet, now relax your feet. Tense up your calves, now relax your calves. Move all the way up the child's body until all the muscles are relaxed.

Visualize

We have all heard the jokes about "going to your happy place" and while there is a bit of truth to that concept, this is a bit deeper than that. Have your child choose a memory or dream that would be happy and calming. That recent trip to the play park might be too stimulating, but a walk along the beach would be perfect. Have your child come up with the idea or at least agree to one that you think of. Then have your child remember or dream that scene using all of his senses. What does it look like? What does it smell like" What does it feel like on your skin? What sounds do you hear?

I often use floating in the waves in Southern California. This is an old memory as I live in Oregon where the waves are much too cold without a wet suit.

I imagine:

- The sensation of the waves moving my body gently up and down.

- The salty water in the back of my throat.

- The sound of the sea gulls and the waves crashing on the shore.

- The sun on my head

- The slightly fishy, salty smell

- The sight of blue sky with the white puffy clouds and the greenish water

This memory is a very powerful and very calming for me. The more senses that you get involved the better. By using all your senses, your mind will become very busy with this wonderful memory or dream and will not have any space for racing thoughts or worries. Have some fun with this and see what I mean.

Sweet dreams!

Self Esteem: the real deal

There's been a myriad of articles and even whole books written regarding the importance of self-esteem, how to build self-esteem, and whether there is really such a thing as self esteem. It can be quite confusing for a parent who is concerned about raising a child into a healthy and well-adjusted adult.

Dictionary.com defines Self Esteem as:

1.a realistic respect for or favorable impression of oneself; self-respect. 2.an inordinately or exaggeratedly favorable impression of oneself.

And they report that the word originates from Phrenology—the study of analyzing the bumps on a person's head to discover various attributes about that person.

Yikes, no wonder Self Esteem seems to have so much baggage attached to it. It means both a realistic as well as exaggeratedly favorable impression of oneself? How can that be? (sigh)

So, for this reason I tend to shy away from using this word at all. I will use Self Confidence instead often, but the bottom line is that we all want our kids to have a realistic idea about what a great kid they are. I believe that by having that special knowledge your child will be more self-confident as they move through the world.

So, how can you help your child to have a realistic idea about him or herself? Here are some ideas:

1.**Encourage a variety of adventures.** Allow your child to try to do as many different activities as they have interest in trying plus a few that they are not so sure about. Some easy things in addition to very challenging things will give your child a chance to shine.

2.**Praise your child specifically.** You have heard me talk about this in the first chapter. This is not empty compliments or general "good job" comments, but praising specific things that your child is doing in the moment.

3.**Allow your child to fail.** Failure is more important than success in building self esteem. The child who learns to manage their frustration and can get up to try again is building self-confidence and self esteem. It's the hard fought victories that build character.

4.**Encourage effort not outcomes**. Using specific praise to acknowledge the effort your child is putting into a project is much more valuable than that prize that may or may not ever get earned. Persistence is one of the key qualities in success in life—notice it and comment on it.

I hope this shines a little light on the subject of how to build self-esteem in your children.

Conclusion

Okay, this is the basis for what I feel is a complete and effective behavior plan. Following this plan consistently in a way that works for your family is the key to creating a more harmonious relationship with your child and to having a more peaceful home. Putting this into action is not an easy thing, and I recommend that you have a friend help you to problem solve when the going gets tough whether it is your spouse or a family member or friend who is supportive.

Getting support through the process, makes it more likely that you will be able to continue being consistent even when the melt downs are exhausting . . . If you don't have a supportive partner in this process, then please visit my blog at http://www.counselingformoms.com/blog and ask a question or make a comment or email me for a personal reply. I want to help. For more consistent support, consider a parent coaching program designed just for you.

http://www.counselingformoms.com/parentcoaching.htm

But wait there's more

This book is a living document, so with that in mind, I have created a website that will provide you with printable forms and even more information. You will be able to easily interact with me and other parents regarding how to apply these techniques and any others. Here is the site:

http://www.betterbehaviorwithoutstress.com

About the Author

Since 2002, Karen DeBolt has been helping moms struggling with chaos at home who want their children to be happy and successful. Karen has a master's degree in Counseling Psychology with a child and family emphasis.

Even more importantly, she has three master teachers at home— her three children, two who have special needs. Karen has struggled with her own children in the past and was able through a lot of studying, experimenting, counseling and persistence to calm the chaos in her home. Karen is passionate about helping other parents to avoid the long struggle and start enjoying parenting again.

Acknowledgements

There are so many people who I want to thank for helping me with the book either directly or indirectly.

All the therapists who have helped me with my children over the years.

My mom and dad who loved and parented my brother and I so very well without a book like this. My brother who inspired my sibling combat chapter and has been a great supporter since we got over that stage.

My best friends Kathy Harrison, Martha Hyatt, and Arwen Foster for their wise words and support over the years.

My professors and supervisors Faith Winters, Steve Berman, Gordon Lindbloom and Peter Mortola who inspired me and believed in me.

My mastermind partners who truly helped me birth this baby, Siddheshwari Sullivan and Denise Barnes. Sage advice about the process and encouragement that I do have what it takes from Anne Wayman. Kristin and Aaron Hanson who inspired and helped with editing this book and helped me with Day Camp.

Julie Flaming editor extraordinaire who was able to look at it when I just couldn't any more!

Also, my spiritual teachers Sandy Shipley and Mark Silver who helped me to find spiritual nurturance when I was without confidence. David Shipley who taught me so much as alternatives to sleeping medications and a whole lot more!

Most of all I thank my clients who I hope will enjoy this book and through its pages calm the chaos in their homes and not feel so alone while they do.

Bibliography

The Explosive Child: A New Approach for Understanding and Parenting Easily Frustrated, Chronically Inflexible Children by Ross W. Greene (Paperback - Sep 30, 2005)

The Five Love Languages of Children by Gary Chapman and Ross Campbell M.D. (Paperback - June 1, 1997)

The Out-of-Sync Child: Recognizing and Coping with Sensory Processing Disorder, Revised Edition by Carol Stock Kranowitz and Lucy Jane Miller (Paperback - April 4, 2006)

The Out-of-Sync Child Has Fun, Revised Edition: Activities for Kids with Sensory Processing Disorder by Carol Stock Kranowitz (Paperback - Aug 1, 2006)

Thinking About You, Thinking About Me by Michelle Garcia Winner (Paperback - Sep 2007)

Transforming the Difficult Child: The Nurtured Heart Approach by Howard Glasser and Jennifer Easley (Paperback - April 1999)